THE SOFTWARE DESIGN PROCESS

TRY, TRY AGAIN

BARBARA M. LINDE

PowerKiDS press.

New York

Published in 2019 by The Rosen Publishing Group, Inc.
29 East 21st Street, New York, NY 10010

First Edition

Editor: Jane Katirgis
Book Design: Reann Nye

Photo Credits: Cover Maksim Kabakou/Shutterstock.com; p. 5 Rido/Shutterstock.com; p. 6 Georgejmclittle/Shutterstock.com; p. 7 Stokkete/Shutterstock.com; p. 9 baranq/Shutterstock.com; p. 11 Dragon Images/Shutterstock.com; p. 12 HelloRF Zcool/Shutterstock.com; p. 15 nd3000/Shutterstock.com; p. 17 Bloomicon/Shutterstock.com; p. 19 Tom Werner/Taxi/Getty Images; p. 20 Sam Edwards/Caiaimage/Getty Images; p. 21 Melody Smart/Shutterstock.com; p. 23 Dean Drobot/Shutterstock.com; p. 25 Hill Street Studios/Blend Images/Getty Images; p. 26 SCIENCE SOURCE/Getty Images; p. 27 https://commons.wikimedia.org/wiki/File:Dennis_Ritchie_(right)_Receiving_Japan_Prize.jpeg; p. 29 Tyler Olson/Shutterstock.com; p. 30 espies/Shutterstock.com.

Library of Congress Cataloging-in-Publication Data

Names: Linde, Barbara M., author.
Title: The software design process : try, try again / Barbara M. Linde.
Description: New York : PowerKids Press, [2019] | Series: Essential concepts in computer science | Includes bibliographical references and index.
Identifiers: LCCN 2017050175| ISBN 9781538331736 (library bound) | ISBN 9781538331743 (pbk.) | ISBN 9781538331750 (6 pack)
Subjects: LCSH: Software engineering—Juvenile literature. | Application software—Development—Juvenile literature.
Classification: LCC QA76.758 .L5234 2019 | DDC 005.1—dc23
LC record available at https://lccn.loc.gov/2017050175

Manufactured in the United States of America

CPSIA Compliance Information: Batch #CS18PK: For Further Information contact Rosen Publishing, New York, New York at 1-800-237-9932

CONTENTS

THE DESIGN PROCESS 4

HARDWARE AND SOFTWARE 6

A SOFTWARE DESIGNER'S JOB. 8

A SOFTWARE ENGINEER'S JOB 10

THE SOFTWARE DEVELOPMENT
   LIFE CYCLE 12

STEP 1: PLANNING THE PROJECT 14

STEP 2: DEFINING THE PROGRAM 16

STEP 3: DESIGNING THE
   PRODUCT ARCHITECTURE. 18

STEP 4: BUILDING THE PROGRAM 20

STEP 5: TESTING THE SOFTWARE 22

STEP 6: DEPLOYING THE SOFTWARE. 24

FAMOUS SOFTWARE ARCHITECTS 26

YOU CAN BE A SOFTWARE DESIGNER 28

HELPFUL TIPS. 30

GLOSSARY 31

INDEX 32

WEBSITES 32

THE DESIGN PROCESS

Have you ever drawn a picture of a slick sports car or a spacecraft? Perhaps you have drawn a new toy or a fancy playhouse. Have you written a story and planned the cover and the illustrations? Then you have **designed** something. Designers get an idea. Then they create a plan that can be made into something.

A **process** is a series of actions that lead to a finished product. You use the writing process when you write a report or a story. You use another process when you follow a recipe to cook or bake something.

Computers need software **programs** to work. Talented people called software designers imagine and create these programs. Read on to find out what they do and how they do it.

COMPUTER CONNECTION
The word *computer* was first used around 1613. Originally, it meant a person who worked with numbers, such as doing addition or subtraction.

Software designers often work in teams as they develop programs.

5

HARDWARE AND SOFTWARE

A computer system uses hardware and software. The case, keyboard, monitor, tower, and mouse are all hardware. You can see and touch them. The hard drive, motherboard, fan, and other pieces inside the computer case are also part of the hardware. You can see them if you open the computer case.

Software is the set of instructions that tell the computer hardware what to do. System software, such as

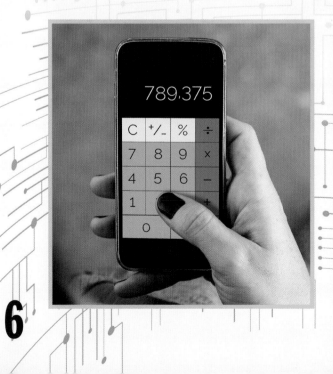

WHAT'S AN APP?

There are many types of apps. A word processing program lets the user type letters or reports. A calculator adds, subtracts, and does other math problems. There are apps for email and checking the weather. Internet search apps are great for doing research. Libraries have apps that let readers download books onto personal computers. Don't forget all the game apps!

Computer software includes applications, or apps, that help the computer do a specific task.

the computer's **operating system**, tells the hardware and the other software how to work together. This software is on the computer when you buy it. Application software, or apps, do specific jobs on the computer. You can download or **install** software on your computer. Network software lets several computers talk to each other.

A SOFTWARE DESIGNER'S JOB

A software designer designs, creates, and tests software. The software might be used in computers for businesses, hospitals, or schools. It could be used in computer games. Scientists need software, too. So do people who make television shows and movies.

The designers figure out what the software needs to do and how to do it. They think about what the computer screen will look like when the software is used.

Some software designers work for large companies. They design the programs that the company needs. Others have their own businesses. They work with many different companies that need specific software. Software designers often telecommute. That means they work from home and log in to a computer that is in an office somewhere else.

WELCOME TO SILICON VALLEY

"Silicon Valley" is a nickname for an area near San Francisco, California. Silicon is a material used in making computers and computer parts. The valley is the Santa Clara Valley between San Francisco and San Jose. Many computer and technology companies have their offices in Silicon Valley. A lot of important research and development happens there.

8

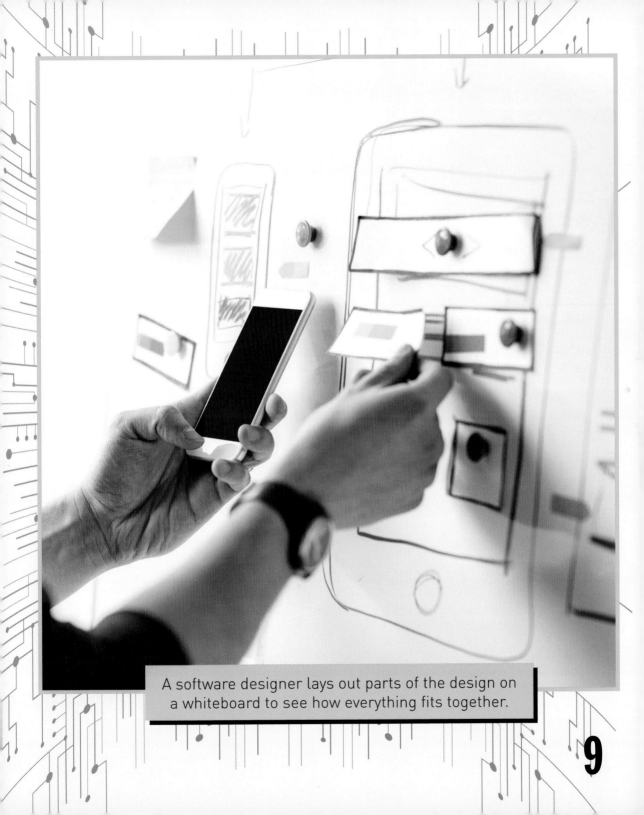

A software designer lays out parts of the design on a whiteboard to see how everything fits together.

9

A SOFTWARE ENGINEER'S JOB

Software engineers spend a lot of time solving problems. Suppose a business has a software program, but they need it to do something that it doesn't already do. Software engineers understand how the program works. They can figure out how to change the software to do the new work. The engineer might also help to create new software.

Part of the software engineer's job might be to teach people how to use the software. To do this, software engineers need to be able to explain things clearly. They might need a lot of patience, too.

A systems software engineer is in charge of all of the software for a company. An applications software engineer works on specific programs.

In 2017, the average annual salary for a software engineer was about $100,000.

11

THE SOFTWARE DEVELOPMENT LIFE CYCLE

When software designers create software, they use a process. This process is called the Software Development Life Cycle, or SDLC. It's a plan that tells developers how to create and develop software and keep it in good shape. The plan also explains how to go about fixing or changing software when it gets out of date. The steps in the process are always the same.

The SDLC can be used with different types and sizes of projects. Following the same steps with every new

COMPUTER CONNECTION
The United States has more than 100,000 software and information technology (IT) companies. These companies have almost two million workers.

DEFINING · PLANNING · DEPLOYMENT · TESTING · BUILDING · DESIGNING

Software designers carefully follow each step in the Software Development Life Cycle.

software program helps development teams make sure that everything is done correctly. Team members can work quickly and still be accurate.

The SDLC might take weeks, months, or even years to complete. The steps are planning, defining, designing, building, testing, and **deployment**. Read more about each step in the following pages.

13

STEP 1: PLANNING THE PROJECT

Members of the design team meet with the **client**. The team and the client brainstorm together. They trade ideas and talk about what the client wants. Team members ask questions: *Why is the software needed? What do you need the software to do? Who will use the software? How much do the users know about computers? How many computers will need the software? How expensive can the software be?*

The design team uses the information to plan how they will design the software. They might have more questions for the client, or the client may have questions for them. The team will probably make several drafts of their plan. They will work until they think they have the best plan.

DEALING WITH DEADLINES

When your teacher tells you that your book report is due in one week, you have a deadline. Software designers have many deadlines as they work. There are deadlines for each part of the process, and a final deadline. The design team leader keeps a calendar and checks in with everyone to see how the work is going. When necessary, changes are made to the schedule.

The software development team meets with a client. Together, they plan the software program.

STEP 2: DEFINING THE PROGRAM

The software designers **define** the software system requirements. They write down all of the details. These include what the software system has to do and how it will work. The design team uses words, numbers, and drawings to explain the process. They break the whole job into smaller parts. Doing this helps them figure out who will work on the different parts during the rest of the process. Team members make several drafts of their work. They work until they are satisfied.

If the client wants to see the final document, team leaders show it to them. The client approves the plans or asks for changes. If there are changes, the team makes them and shows the new document to the client.

Software designers think about how the program will work. They imagine what the user will see on the computer monitor. **>**

17

STEP 3: DESIGNING THE PRODUCT ARCHITECTURE

When you see the word "architecture," you probably think of plans for buildings or styles of buildings. However, when we're talking about computers, "architecture" means the design of the software program. It's the process that the designer uses to figure out how to create the program. The designer makes decisions about the parts of the program, what each part does, and how the parts work together.

If you try to build a building without a plan, you would have a very hard time. The building might fall down, or you might not be able to build it at all. Creating a software program without the architecture works the same way. The designers might not put in all of the parts, or they could create a program that's too hard to use.

Developers often collaborate, or work together, to design the architecture.

STEP 4: BUILDING THE PROGRAM

Now it's the computer programmer's turn. The programmers take the designer's plan and make the software program. They do this by writing **code**. Code is a set of instructions that the computer's hardware can understand. These instructions have to be exact, so the computer does the right thing.

Code is written in different computer languages. The programmer learns to use these languages. It's a lot

COMPUTER PROGRAMMERS

Computer programming is a good job if you like to work alone and you can pay close attention to details. Many programmers work from home, since they spend most of their time at the computer. Most programmers know several computer languages. The average salary for a programmer is about $80,000.

```
<body>
<div class="main">
<div class="header">
<div class="block_header">
<div class="logo"><a href="index.html"...
<div class="menu">
<ul>
<li><a href="index.html"><span>...
<li><a href="services.html"...
<li><a href="services.html"...
<li><a href="portfolio.html"...
<li><a href="contact.html"...
</ul>
</div>
..."clr"></div>
```

This program is written in HTML, or hypertext markup language. This language is used to create the pages you see on the Internet.

like learning to speak a new language, such as Spanish, Chinese, or French.

Each type of software program uses a certain language. For example, if programmers are designing software to use on the web, they would likely write it in JavaScript. Coding for video games most often uses the C language. YouTube and Google are both written partially with Python.

STEP 5: TESTING THE SOFTWARE

Would you test a new bicycle before you bought it? Do you test a sample of a video game before you buy it? In much the same way, software designers test their product. They do this to make sure the software does what it's supposed to do, the way it's supposed to do it. Testing also makes sure there aren't any bugs in the software.

Several people test the software and record what they find. Someone from the design team might test it first. Next, someone who is not familiar with the software tests it. There are tests on several computers, too. Programmers fix any bugs and retest the software. The design team will try, try again until they are happy with the test results.

COMPUTER CONNECTION

Software testers often take classes to prepare for their job. They get a certification if they pass the course's test. This lets them get good-paying jobs as testers.

Software designers check for bugs and debug the code as necessary.

23

STEP 6: DEPLOYING THE SOFTWARE

At last, the software program is ready to go. It's deployed, or released to the client. The client or someone from the software company installs the program on the client's computer. The client starts using it. There may be additional revisions and fixes if necessary.

This isn't the end of the cycle, though. The software program has to be **maintained**. The users might find out that they need the software to do more things, or they might want some things taken out of the program. Maintenance might include **upgrading** the system. Upgrades allow the program to run faster and to handle more tasks at one time. It's a continuous process.

COMPUTER CONNECTION

If you're using software applications on your home computer, you might get notices for upgrades. Directions appear on the monitor that lead you through the steps to make the upgrade.

It is exciting when the new software program is up and running!

FAMOUS SOFTWARE ARCHITECTS

REAR ADMIRAL DR. GRACE MURRAY HOPPER (1906–1992)

When Dr. Grace Murray Hopper was in the Navy during World War II, she was one of the first women to work with computers. After the war, she worked with a team that created one of the first computer languages. In 1991, Hopper was the first woman to receive the U.S. National Medal of Technology.

COMPUTER BUGS

Once when a computer wasn't working, Dr. Hopper's team found a moth in it. On September 9, 1947, she wrote in the logbook, "First actual case of bug being found." The term "bug" for a computer problem stuck. Now people talk about computer bugs and debugging computers all the time.

26

In 2011, Dr. Ritchie (right) and Kenneth Thompson were given the Japan Prize for Information and Communication, honoring their work with Unix.

DR. DENNIS RITCHIE (1941–2011)

Dr. Dennis Ritchie was a computer scientist and a researcher. He created the C language. This language lets the programmer tell the computer what to do. It's the most-used of all computer languages. He worked with another computer scientist to develop the Unix operating system. Ritchie earned many awards, including the U.S. National Medal of Technology in 1998.

YOU CAN BE A SOFTWARE DESIGNER

Would you like to be a software designer? Are you willing to try, try again? Start now to find out. Read books about careers with computers. Talk with software designers and computer programmers. Some websites teach coding just for kids. There are also computer games that teach coding as you play.

Join or start a computer club at school. Study hard in math, science, and reading. When you get to high school, take lots of computer science classes. Math courses, such as algebra, geometry, and calculus, are important, too. So are chemistry and physics. English classes will teach you how to write well.

In college, get a bachelor's degree in computer science. You might want to study more. You could get a master's degree, or even a doctorate.

Learn all you can about computers. They're going to be around for a long time.

HELPFUL TIPS

Use these tips from software designers if you create a program.

PLAN FOR ERRORS. Think about what to do if something unexpected happens. Have a plan so the whole system won't crash.

TEST, TEST, TEST. Get someone to try to break the program. Fix any problems before the software is finished.

MAKE THE SOFTWARE EASY TO USE. The user should be able to install and upgrade the program with no problems.

DOCUMENT EVERYTHING. Take notes about what you are doing and why you are doing it. You can use these notes when you write up the directions.

The software design process takes time and involves trial and error, but the effort is worthwhile. When designers try, try again, users get a smoothly working software program.

GLOSSARY

client: A company or a person who hires a business to do something.

code: The lines of text or symbols used to create a computer program.

define: To use details to describe something clearly.

deployment: To set up something so it is ready to use.

design: To create the plan for something.

install: To set something up to be used; to put a program onto a computer's hard drive.

maintain: To keep something working correctly.

operating system: The software that controls a computer's main functions or business.

process: A series of actions that lead to a result or end.

program: A set of instructions for computer hardware. Also called software.

upgrade: To replace software with a newer or better version.

INDEX

A
application software engineer, 10
apps, 6, 7
architecture, 18, 19

B
bugs, 23, 26

C
client, 14, 15, 24
code, 20, 23
computer languages, 20, 21, 26, 27
computer programmer, 20
computer science, 28

D
deadlines, 14
debugging, 23, 26
deployment, 13, 24

H
hardware, 6, 20
Hopper, Grace Murray, 26
hypertext markup language (HTML),
    20, 21

N
network software, 7

O
operating system, 7

P
program, 4, 6, 30

R
Ritchie, Dennis, 27

S
Silicon Valley, 8
software designer, 4, 8, 13, 14, 16, 23,
    28, 30
Software Development Life Cycle, 12, 13
software engineer, 10, 11
systems software engineer, 10

T
teams, 5, 13, 14
testing, 22, 30

U
Unix operating system, 27

WEBSITES

Due to the changing nature of Internet links, PowerKids Press has developed an online list of websites related to the subject of this book. This site is updated regularly. Please use this link to access the list: www.powerkidslinks.com/eccs/swdes